Restless Spirit

Kristen Rohde

BookLeaf
Publishing

Presentation by *BookLeaf Publishing*

Web: www.bookleafpub.com

E-mail: info@bookleafpub.com

ISBN: 978-93-95755-29-0

First edition 2022

PREFACE

Thank you for picking up this book and taking the time to engage with the Spirit through these few poems.

Walking the Christian walk isn't always easy, in fact it's peppered with challenges and moments of confusion and weariness. God didn't promise it would be easy though, and the reason we don't feel comfortable here is because we weren't created for this world. It's no wonder we're restless when our final destination is yet to be discovered; we're simply detouring here and God-willing making an impact an those around us.

While our struggles are real, our eyes remain set on the Father, our hand is securely held by Jesus, and we're guided by the Spirit through our short time here. May we always look for ways to lift each other up, be bold in our faith, and run the race set before us until we reach the end and hear the words, "Well done, good and faithful servant".

Love, peace & blessings.

God Chose You

God chose you.
He chose you before you chose Him.
He knew that you would be His hands,
His feet,
To a world that just wants to compete.
He knew where you would be,
Who you would see,
And the kind of place he would be sending you
into.
So since He chose you,
He's placed within you
A spirit of kindness, gentleness, and
perseverance to hold to
When this world does not give you
A secure place to return to.
He has never left you alone
To trudge through the coldness alone.
He has allowed you to build your life around
Him,
To build your life on His promises,
On His goodness,
On His faithfulness.
To be a Christ-light to the people you meet,
The people you don't want to meet,
And the people who don't want to meet you.
In our world right now that suffocates

And fluctuates
And likes to debate and pontificate.
We must break in to the hardened and cold
hearts,
The ones that surround us every day
And make us feel like we're not okay
To display to them that our lives are built on a
rock
A strong, steady rock.
So strong that when the wind blows, and the
seas billow
We will never be shaken
And we will stand our ground.
Because we were chosen
And we were enveloped in the arms
Of a God who has spoken
And kept open
His door for those who are broken.
We have been chosen.
And positioned for greatness.
So when we're judged for being different,
When we don't walk to the beat of the world,
Or the values that we've held and exercised
Are criticised and minimised,
We can stand proud and tall and strong
Knowing that our lives have been built upon
God's love.
Love that is a firm foundation.

What If?

The Word says that You are Lord.
It says that You are merciful,
That You are kind,
That You created the universe from nothing
While never losing count of the hairs on my
head.
The Word says that You saved us,
That You pulled us from the miry clay
And reclaimed us for Your glory.
The Word says that You're a light for our path,
A lamp to our feet.
You're a home to the homeless.
Joy to the joyless.
Power to the powerless.
You are God.
What if we really knew this?
That when we spoke to You, we connected to
You.
When we worshipped You, we enjoyed You.
When we sought You, we found You.
What if we really knew?
How the God who changes us
And rearranges us
Is the same God who saved us
From the sin that estranged us.

And we felt the intimacy of a relationship with
the same God
Who never stopped loving us when we thought
He had forgotten us.
What if that division we feel
Is really a bridge that we envision,
An action, a step, a reconnection, not a
supposition.
What if it became more than just religion?
What if you just wanted our affection?
What if we really believe that You are good?
What if we really believe that You are who You
say You are?
King of Kings.
Lord of Lords.
Adonai.
El-Shaddai.
What if You are?
What if?

Be Still

Fear.
Courage.
Two feelings on opposite ends of the spectrum,
Yet how they become entwined in our everyday
lives.
We don't want fear
We want courage.
We want to be courageous.
But when fear creeps in and whispers our name
We hide and miss the opportunity to be
courageous.
We hide behind the belief that fear is an
encompassing shadow,
A ball and chain around our ankles.
But fear is a choice.
Fear is when we believe that God is not with us,
That we are alone.
You of little faith.
God did not promise our lives would be free of
trouble,
That just because we know Him, we're free of
opposition.
No, he said "In this world you will have
trouble".
But take heart

You of little faith.
Did you not know that God has promised,
He's promised He will fight for you,
You need only to be still.
So be still, little flock.
The presence of God is all around.
He will never leave you, never forsake you,
never give up on you,
He is always with you.
Be still.
Because when the time comes
For you to fight or flee,
Exchange your fear for faith
And see courage be a shield as you walk into the
deepest unknown.
Grace.
It's what tells us that God is always present,
It's what shows us that God always provides,
It's what encourages us that God's Spirit
empowers us,
It's what reminds us that our life is purposeful,
And it's the promise of Immanuel, I AM WITH
YOU.
Be still.
The Lord will fight for you.
You need only to be still.

Do you know who you are?

Do you know who you are?
Do you know whose you are?
Can your mind comprehend who moulded you
like clay,
Who knit your bones together,
Who knew every inch of your body, your
character, your mind
Even before the very foundations of the earth?
Do you know who placed you in this moment, in
this age, for such a time as this?
Do you question who you are?
Do you ever question whose you are?
Can you say for sure that the mind of God can
be comprehended?
His thoughts reach far beyond the limitations of
earth.
His ways can never be predicted.
Yet his voice, a mere whisper, can break the
barriers of heaven and earth
To meet you here, now, in this moment, in this
age, for such a time as this.
When those valleys are far greater than the
mountains,
When your thoughts are a contortion of fear and
anger and disbelief,

When you know that the deepest part of your heart
couldn't be bruised any more,
When you relive yesterday, last week, last year,
Dwell on tomorrow, next week, next year,
Until you don't have any more "todays" left.
The constant, the predictable, the everyday moments
of this world
Are never going to sustain you.
These things are fleeting.
So be gone yesterday, tomorrow, last week, next
week.
Remain steadfast, unmoving, and trusting in now, in
this moment, in this age, for such a time as this.
The Lord has his hand upon you,
He never takes it off,
He never turns away,
He never shifts his loving, embracing, longing gaze
from your face
Because you are royalty.
You are not an impoverished prodigal.
Straighten your crown, daughter of the King.
Lift your eyes, daughter of the King.
Take in the beauty and the wonder and the pure,
unfailing love of a Father who loves you and wants
you and seeks you, even when the valley has
swallowed you.
Know who you are.
Know whose you are.
And live today as who you were created to be.

Faith

Faith is a choice.
It's a choice to choose something different,
Something more than being self-sufficient.
Faith is hard.
It's not something we just get as believers
The minute we say yes to Jesus.
It's choosing to believe that we're held in
something profound
Where favour and mercies abound,
Where miracles are found,
Where people are raised from the ground.
Faith is more than a feeling.
It's more than something appealing.
Something to take when we need it
And forget when we don't.
How often do we doubt it?
How often do our fears remove us from the foot
of God's throne
And lead us to do life alone.
Do you doubt that God wants to take care of
you?
That He doesn't have time for you?
That He isn't there for you?
That your faith isn't enough to get you through?
The size of your faith doesn't matter.

The tiniest of faith can make fear scatter.
It can say to the mountain to move
And that heartbeat inside you proves
A man thought you were worth a sacrifice.
And that you were never meant to take control
of your life.
See faith gives us peace,
Faith gives us courage,
Faith gives us grace and mercy
On the days when we're thirsty
For more of God's goodness, His faithfulness,
His kindness.
Faith is lifting up our eyes.
It's running for the prize.
It's stepping out of the boat
Yet staying afloat
Because our eyes are on Jesus.
On what He can do
Not on what we can't do.
Faith is a choice.
And Jesus is waiting for you.

Graves into Gardens

Unlovable.
Irredeemable.
"Your past is a reflection of your future," the world says.
"Your past cannot be changed and neither can you," the world says.
Unusable.
Insignificant.
"Do you want fame?" the world says.
"Do you want significance?" the world says.
"Follow me and I'll show you how to fit in."
And yet the fame, the glory, the praise, the likes
Are empty and hollow and leave you craving, desiring.
Where to go for more? Who will give you more?
Who will satisfy the unending need for love, for attention, for that deep dark hole in your heart to be filled?
Graves into gardens.
A whisper.
Shame into glory.
A gentle whisper.
And your heart is awakened.
Your soul is moving.
Unlovable?

Beauty from ashes.
Irredeemable?
Mourning to dancing.
Unusable?
Seas into highways.
Insignificant?
Bones into armies.
You who are crushed by despair, overwhelmed
by depression, shaken by fear
Will receive a crown in exchange for ashes,
Gladness in place of sorrow,
You'll be wrapped in victory, joy and praise,
And you'll be lifted higher than the valleys.
You will be called magnificent, like a great
towering tree,
Standing in victory, standing for truth
Standing to the glory of the Eternal who planted
you.
And you will find
That under the wings of the Father
You are…
Loved
Redeemed
Useable
Significant

Jireh

Don't let your hearts be troubled.
Don't let them be troubled in this time of chaos
And not in this time of confusion.
Set your heart on Jehovah Jireh;
The Lord will provide.
Throw away those things of old
Whatever has tied you to the world
In dependence and trust in unreliable stuff.
Set your heart on Jehovah Jireh;
The Lord will provide.
Collect the moments that make you smile
When you were led out of the valley
When you were high up on the mountain
When you were pulled from the mire.
Set your heart on Jehovah Jireh;
The Lord will provide.
The storm won't last as long
When you don't try to see beyond the clouds.
When you don't hide and wait for it to pass
And worry your head that you're alone.
Set your heart on Jehovah Jireh;
The Lord will provide.
Be courageous in the face of persecution,
Be bold in the face of fear,
Be brave when you feel abandoned,

Because God has never been closer
Than in your weakest moment.
He's forever enough.
Always enough.
More than enough.
Jehovah Jireh;
The Lord will provide.

Peace

What is peace?
Is it a state of mind?
Is it a feeling?
Is it something to cling to
When the world around us is falling?
What is peace?
Is it an abstract concept?
A perception of ease and comfort?
Is it a thing to be summoned
And beckoned
In those moments of disillusion
And confusion?
Peace.
Peace isn't a thing,
It isn't a feeling,
It isn't a concept,
An appealing.
It isn't there when we need it
And gone when we have comfort.
It isn't pushy and invading,
It isn't fleeting and fading.
It doesn't choose who to land on,
It's not picky and random.
Peace is a person.
Peace came to earth

When the baby was chosen,
When heaven split open,
When the waters were broken,
And the name was spoken:
Jesus.
Prince of Peace.
Sent to the manger to be God,
Fully human,
To identify with us
And purify us
And bring to earth a gift from the Father.
A gift that cannot be bought,
That cannot be sold,
That cannot be exchanged.
The gift that gives when there's nothing left
inside of us
And when we need someone to deliver us.
And the moment that he invited us
To partake in His will for us
That we might see the storm calmed inside of us
When the world is too loud around us.
Peace.
So rest in the name of relief:
Jesus.
Prince of Peace.
"My peace I leave with you,
My peace I give you."

Persecuted Prayer

Lord God our Father,
Our fortress and high tower.
Your eye is on every sparrow
And even more so on Your children.
Though we may feel a disconnect in our Western
world,
You join our hearts with the persecuted,
The tortured,
And those who feel like they're cornered.
So I pray we feel the desire,
The unrelenting desire,
To fall to our knees with our heads bowed low
For the brothers and sisters on their knees
Finding themselves on death row.
May we come together and seek You
Knowing our family would do anything
To defend You.
The secrecy, the bondage, the lack of freedom to
love You.
We don't know what that's like,
To be threatened with torture and death
When asked if we follow You,
To stand up and say "I do."
Knowing the name we bear
And the faith we share
Is the very thing that leads our brothers and sisters

To their end.
Though thousands of miles away Lord
Our persecuted family is in our hearts.
We share the same heartbeat for You,
And the same passion for You.
Let the freedom we have
Be what we need to take Your name
Further than it is right now.
To the streets, the city, the nation.
And while we have this freedom
Let us realise the blessing we have
To share Your name,
Speak Your name,
Lift up Your name.
And let it be known that Your name
Is what will remain
When heaven and earth fade
And we finally come face to face
And heart to heart
With the One who was worth it.
Lord we pray and seek Your favour today.
Bring comfort, peace, strength and resilience
To those willing to sacrifice their lives for You.
And give us the grace and ability to sacrifice what it
is we have
For you.
For You are our cornerstone.
Christ alone.

Rejoice

Rejoice!
Again I say, rejoice!
See the love brought down from the Father,
The little baby in the manger.
See how he cries, whimpers and smiles,
See his tiny hands, his feet
Helpless and fragile.
See how he's already worshipped
Though fresh from the womb.
This baby, a Godsend,
To be Saviour of all.
So rejoice, children of God
Again, I say rejoice!
Your sins do not have to weigh you down,
You are true royalty and you were gifted that
crown.
Jesus was born with one thing in mind
To honour his Father,
To identify with his brother
And to spread the message to love one another.
He did not come to be the highlight,
His intention wasn't to glory in the limelight.
He humbled himself among sinners, thieves, and
the poor,
Because he wants us to know

That he loves us without question.
That was his intention.
So rejoice in the Lord.
Rejoice in His faithfulness.
Rejoice in His kindness.
Rejoice in His goodness.
Rejoice.
And again I say rejoice.

Victory

Why must the things of this world,
The things that I hate the most,
That I don't want the most,
That I struggle with the most,
Be the things that I gravitate towards?
My brain only telling me they're rewards.
Why do I keep doing
What I don't want to do?
Keep sinning
When I know there's a better way through.
We remain captive by our thoughts
Our flesh, our desires.
Pulled the wrong way
By the things that entice us
And we can't see beyond the captivity.
The fact that we're really empty
And damaging our connectivity
With Christ's divinity.
I know that I'm so much more than this.
I'm more than my failure,
I'm more than my mistakes,
I'm more than my weakness.
Because there is One who takes my weakness
And places inside of me the heart of a lioness.
And the giants before me

Are no longer greater than me.
The demons ahead of me
Scatter around me.
And the roar of a lioness wells up inside of me
Knowing that the One who gives me strength
Has always come to my defence
And pleaded my case for victory.
I'm not a failure no matter how many times I
fail.
God knew who He was creating
And His plan for me will continue to prevail.
So I'll straighten my crown,
I'll sharpen my sword,
And I'll believe His word,
That His love will never fail.

Whom shall I send?

"Whom shall I send?
Who will go for me?"
The Lord sees His people and the ripe harvest
around us.
He declares, in our hearts, that we must move.
We must awake from our slumber and move
forth to what is before us.
"Whom shall I send?
Who will go for me?"
His eyes roam the earth.
They see the lost,
They see the downcast, the broken, the hearts of
stone
Yet they are still His children, separated from the
flock.
Their hearts long for something deeper,
Something more profound,
Something more vivid and sincere and steadfast.
And the Lord's heart aches for them.
"Whom shall I send?
Who will go for me?"
The Lord's people are awakened.
They see the need, the full harvest, the
overflowing vats
And like an army rising up

They don't come to conquer but to heal.
To heal a land that has been poisoned with the
sting of sin
To heal the hearts of those who have followed
the broad road
To bind up the broken hearted,
Proclaim good news to the poor,
Freedom for the prisoners,
Sight for the blind,
And freedom from oppression.
The mission field is before us
Wherever we are, whoever we see, whatever we
do.
The harvest is bountiful, yet the labourers are
few.
"Whom shall I send?
Who will go for me?"

You are still God

When the sun falls
And the night takes over.
When one day ends
And another begins,
You are still God.
When sleep evades us,
And the enemy degrades us,
When fear swells around us,
And our worries hold onto us,
You are still God.
Above all and through all,
Our Maker within all,
You are constantly kind,
Consistent,
Persistent.
On the days when we love You,
We seek You,
We find You,
You are still God.
On the days when we hurt You,
Disobey You,
Ignore You,
When we think we don't need You
Though we've got nothing to cling to,
You are still God.

No one can change what is unchangeable.
No one can move what is immovable.
So we find You as our hiding place,
Our safe refuge.
We find You on the mountain tops
And down in the valleys.
We find You in heartbreak,
In pandemics,
Epidemics,
In joy, sadness, and the inauthentic.
You are still God.
The same God who sheds a light
On our darkest thoughts.
The God who dries our tears
When we thought He'd forgot.
The God who calls us worthy
When we think that we're not.
You are the same,
Yesterday, today and forever.
You are still God.

Home

We were not made for here.
This place is not our home.
We were not created to adhere
To the rules of this world
And be consumed by fear.
We were made for so much more.
More than we can ever imagine,
Than we can ever comprehend,
And yet we're caught in this war
Between good and evil,
Distractions and commitments,
Chaos and contentment.
And when we look around
And see the entanglement of sin
We can remember we are beyond that,
If we simply remember the blood of Jesus.
This place is not our home.
If we feel discontent on a daily basis
We can be sure we're not home
And we're not trying to reach it on our own.
We can rest in the guidance of the Spirit,
The reach of the Father,
And the promise of Jesus
That we'll finally stand before the throne
And find our permanent home.

Do you hear the chains?

Do you hear the chains?
Shaking against the walls, unbreaking,
unmoving.
Bound like prisoners, suffering under the hand
of the enemy,
The one who wants us to bleed, to cry, to suffer
Because we bear the name of the King.
Do you hear the chains?
The ones that hold you, that bind you, that you
shake against the walls.
Do you feel the weight of the chains pulling you
back?
You think you're free, then they pull you back.
Bound in fear.
Bound in sadness.
Bound in shame.
Bound in guilt.
Bound in emptiness.
Bound in unrelenting thoughts that nothing will
change,
The world won't change,
People won't change.
Will they? Will we?
Who will move first?
Who will stand against the captivity?

So in faith, we stand.
Do you hear the chains?
They're breaking.
And so another stands,
And another,
And another,
Until there's an army
All speaking one name:
The name of Jesus
Do you hear the chains?
They're breaking.
Falling.
We step forward, another step, and another, until
nothing can stop us.
Together, picking each other up, holding hands,
facing the prison door
And we move as we feel the Spirit, as one army,
as one people,
Speaking the name of Jesus.
Drawing on the power of Jesus.
Do you hear the chains?
They fall to the ground.
Prisoners released from the darkness,
Delivered from the hand of the enemy,
And lifted high upon the hilltop with a victory,
With a sense of hope,
And the strength of a thousand armies
All resting in the powerful name of Jesus.

Gospel Prayer

Lord God our Father
You have stretched your hand over Your
children today
Desiring that our hearts would be prepared,
Engaged,
And eager to be filled with what You have to
say.
We've all come from a week of stuff;
Busyness.
Happiness.
Painfulness.
Sadness.
Joyfulness.
You know each of our circumstances.
You know what we've needed and what we've
been full of.
You know what situations made us crave you
And what situations made us mad at you.
You didn't leave one of us alone
To do our week on our own.
Your hand was within each situation,
No matter how we may have felt,
How we may have portrayed you
Or betrayed you,

Regardless… You are working in our
circumstances right in this moment.
Because You knew they were going to happen
Before they even happened.
Because you have called us into your beloved
family
And life with You is our reality.
Which means we no longer go through life alone
Because we are fully loved and fully known.
But Lord Your love is not just for us.
It's not a form of comfort,
Something to keep and use when we need it,
It's a gift for us and a gift for the lost.
We are often tempted to hold it tight
Because we feel that we deserved it
And we fear that we might lose it,
Our possessiveness making us indignant.
But You never planned for Your love to be
stagnant.
Help us be deliverers of Your Word,
Grace us with courage to release our grip
And open our mouths so it would be heard
Among those who don't understand You
Or have a misconception of You.
So that when the time comes
For You to gather Your children home
You would say of those who were lost,
"They're coming home,
Because You, child, were brave enough

Not to hold My love alone."
Help us see how valuable the gospel is,
And what our duty is
To carry out and not to ignore,
To take it beyond our four walls.
In the precious name of Jesus,
Amen.

You are Safe

You are held so close, did you know?
The arms wrapped around you
Are not of a human touch,
A fallible human touch.
You are wrapped in the arms of a divine being
Far greater, far stronger, far sweeter
Than anything you could imagine for yourself.
Why do you fight against those arms?
Why do you press against the comfort
That reminds you of safety?
You know you're not in control,
Nothing in your life is in your control.
Nothing you can see, or touch, or hear, or smell
Will ever provide the kind of comfort
That the arms of the Father provide.
Relax yourself into them
And feel the closeness of the Father's embrace.
Invite the divine presence to enclose you
And keep you warm.
Don't be afraid.
You don't need to be afraid.
You've got all you need in your Father.

Take Heart

A heart of heaviness,
A sinking feeling that won't subside.
A feeling of weariness,
And a burden of fearfulness that steals your
joyfulness.
Oh, those are the things that create seeds of
doubt.
Is God still there?
Does He still see me?
Has He forgotten me?
Does He not exist to me,
Anymore?
Amidst the tears and the anguish,
Crying out to the Father,
From where you began to where you are now,
But no answer can be heard.
Why has He abandoned me?
Why has He forsaken me?
Don't forget that the words of Jesus
Were the same words you speak in your pain.
Yet He believed and He trusted and He released
His pain
To the One whose heart bled as He watched His
Son die.
Take heart, wandering flock,

The Lord is closer than you think.
In fact, He's closer than He's been before,
You just don't let Him past your walls.
He sees the things that make you cry.
The heart of disappointment.
The spirit of discontentment.
The feeling of misalignment.
But the Lord never fails.
The joy of the Lord will prevail.

www.ingramcontent.com/pod-product-compliance
Lightning Source LLC
Chambersburg PA
CBHW061320140726
47998CB00006B/2478